OUR SOLAR SYSTEM

The International Space Station

BY DANA MEACHEN RAU

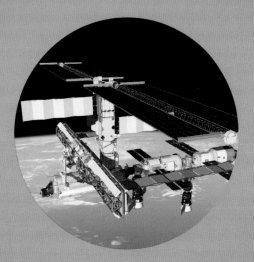

Content Adviser: Dr. Stanley P. Jones, Assistant Director, Washington, D.C., Operations, NASA-Sponsored Classroom of the Future

Science Adviser: Terrence E. Young Jr., M.Ed., M.L.S., Jefferson Parish (Louisiana) Public School System

Reading Adviser: Susan Kesselring, M.A., Literacy Educator, Rosemount-Apple Valley-Eagan (Minnesota) School District

COMPASS POINT BOOKS

MINNEAPOLIS, MINNESOTA

For Charlie and Allison—D.M.R.

Compass Point Books
3109 West 50th Street, #115
Minneapolis, MN 55410

Visit Compass Point Books on the Internet at *www.compasspointbooks.com*
or e-mail your request to *custserv@compasspointbooks.com*

Photographs ©: NASA, cover, 1, 3, 4, 5, 6, 9 (bottom), 11 (all), 12–13, 14 (all), 15, 16, 17 (all), 19, 20 (top), 21, 22, 23, 24, 25, 26, 27, 28–29; Keystone/Getty Images, 9 (top); NASA/Bill Ingalls, 20 (bottom).

Editor: Nadia Higgins
Lead Designer/Page production: The Design Lab
Photo researcher: Svetlana Zhurkina
Educational Consultant: Diane Smolinski

Managing Editor: Catherine Neitge
Art Director: Keith Griffin
Production Director: Keith McCormick
Creative Director: Terri Foley

Library of Congress Cataloging-in-Publication Data
Rau, Dana Meachen, 1971–
  The International Space Station / by Dana Meachen Rau : Nadia Higgins, editor.
      p. cm. — (Our solar system)
  Includes index.
  ISBN 0-7565-0852-5 (hardcover)
  1. International Space Station. I. Higgins, Nadia. II. Title.
  TL797.15.R38 2004
  629.44'2—dc22

2004015570

Table of Contents

High Above Earth

✦ Imagine you are sleeping. Suddenly, you hear soft music over the radio and someone says, "Wake up! You have a busy day ahead!" You open your eyes. You are upside down! You are strapped to a wall in a sleeping bag. When you get out of your bag, you start floating around in the air.

This is not a dream. It is a morning on the International Space Station. The International Space Station, also called the ISS, is a

Microgravity causes people and ▶ things to float around in space.

spacecraft orbiting, or traveling around, Earth. It flies about 220 miles (352 kilometers) above the ground. That's about 36 times as high as an airplane flies. The spacecraft travels at about 17,500 miles (28,000 km) per hour—300 times as fast as a car on the highway.

Astronauts float inside the spacecraft because of microgravity. On Earth, gravity is the force that pulls objects to the ground. In space, astronauts can't feel Earth's pull, so they float while they work and sleep.

◀ Astronaut Susan J. Helms looks out her window at Earth far below.

While the crew is sleeping, the sky is not always dark. It is not always light when they are awake either. As the space station orbits Earth, the sun sets every 90 minutes. Daylight and nighttime last for only 45 minutes each. The crew can't rely on the sun to plan their day. They schedule about 16 hours for work, meals, exercise, and breaks. Then they sleep for about 8 hours.

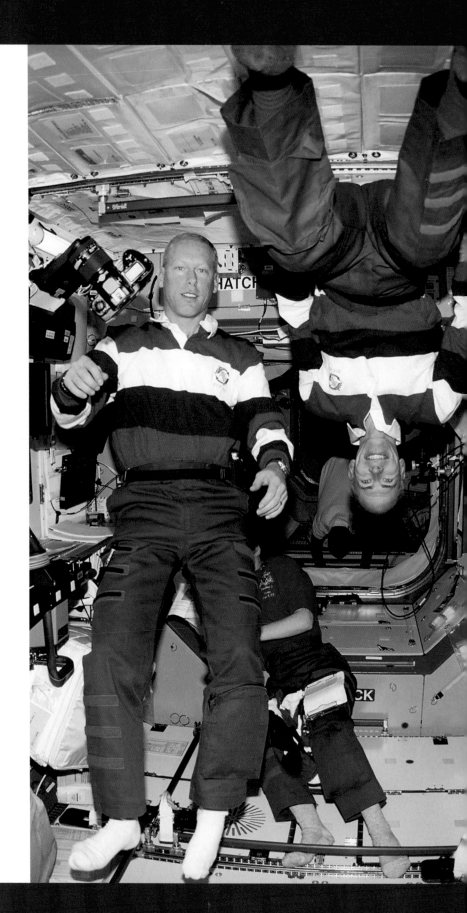

Two astronauts take a break from their work to have some fun with microgravity. ▶

When it is daytime for you, it is nighttime on the other side of Earth. Half of the planet is in sunlight while the other half is in darkness. The sun sets every 90 minutes aboard the International Space Station because that's how long it takes the spacecraft to orbit Earth.

For 45 minutes, the space station is on the side of Earth where the sun is shining and it is daytime. Then for about 45 minutes, it is in darkness as it crosses the side of Earth having night. The sun comes into view again when the station reaches Earth's lit side.

The Need for Space Stations

Since ancient times, people have been watching the skies and making charts of the moon, stars, and planets. They have wondered about Earth and its place in the universe. About 50 years ago, people found ways to send spacecraft into the sky. Unpiloted probes collected information about the moon and planets. Then people began visiting space as well, orbiting Earth and even landing on the moon. Different countries wanted to be the first ones to make important discoveries about space. The United States and the Soviet Union (a nation that later broke up into Russia and other nearby countries) competed in a "space race" for decades.

With each mission, scientists learned more about Earth, the planets, and the stars. Each mission also created more questions. Space stations became a way for astronauts to actually live in space for months at a time. These larger spacecraft gave astronauts the opportunity to answer some of their questions about the universe.

Important Dates in Space Exploration

1957—The Soviet Union launches *Sputnik 1,* the first spacecraft to travel into space.

1961—Yuri Gagarin (1934–1968) from the Soviet Union becomes the first person to travel into space.

1969—American astronauts Neil Armstrong (1930–) and Edwin "Buzz" Aldrin (1930–) land on the moon.

1971—The Soviet Union sends the first space station into orbit. It is called *Salyut 1.*

1973—The United States sends up the space station *Skylab.*

Yuri Gagarin ▲

Buzz Aldrin ▶

continued on page 10

9

continued from page 9

1981—The United States flies the first space shuttle, which is a type of spacecraft that can be used over and over again.

1986—The Russians put the space station *Mir* into orbit.

1995—The United States and Russia begin working together on *Mir.*

1998—Work begins on the International Space Station.

2010—Work on the International Space Station is expected to be completed.

A U.S. space shuttle ▲

The space station Mir ▶

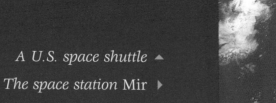

In the 1980s, U.S. President Ronald Reagan (1911–2004) announced his idea for Space Station Freedom. The project later became the International Space Station. The United States would work together with Russia, as well as 14 other countries around the world, to build the space station.

The space station was planned as a way to bring astronauts from different nations together as part of a crew. They would be able to perform experiments in space that could not be done on Earth.

The station would also teach them how to live in space for a long time. This would prepare astronauts for longer missions in the future, including trips to Mars and the moon, where they might someday be able to live and work.

In 1998, work began on the International Space Station. For now, the station is a huge construction site. It is expected to be completed in 2010.

Parts of the Space Station

The International Space Station is somewhat like a building set you might find at the toy store. It has large round pieces, small round pieces, long connecting pieces, and large flat pieces. The parts of the space station are made on Earth. Then a U.S. space shuttle or Russian *Soyuz* spacecraft brings them up to the station.

When the ISS is complete, it will be about as wide as one-and-a-half football fields and

An illustration of how the International Space Station will look upon its expected completion in 2010

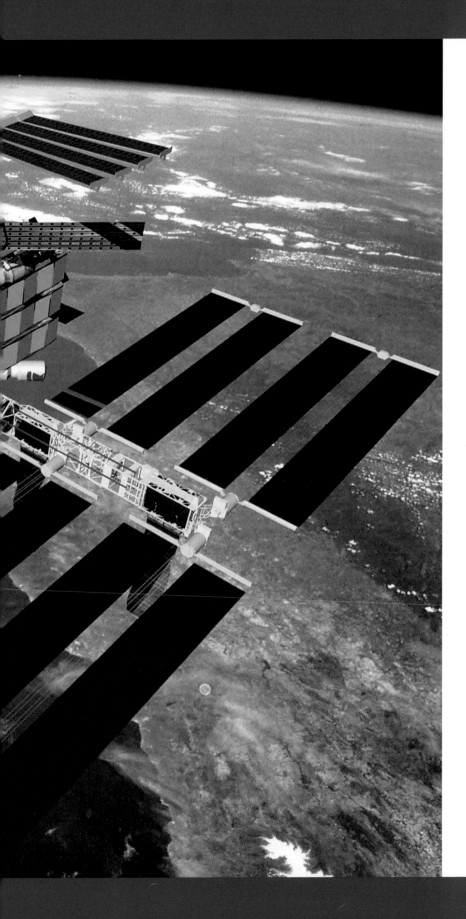

weigh about 500 tons (450 metric tons). The station will have nine main parts where the crew will live and work. These parts, called modules, are like giant tubes. They will form the inner part of the station.

Today, the *Zvezda* Service Module, built by Russia, is where the crew lives. It is also where the crew controls the power, flight, and communication with people on Earth. The U.S.-built *Destiny* laboratory occupies another module. This is where the astronauts do experiments. When the station is finished, it will have six laboratories in all.

You might think the station looks like a giant insect. Large rectangular panels on both sides look like wings, but they aren't. These are solar arrays. They use energy from the sun to make electricity.

Canada created a robotic arm for the station. It is connected near the middle of the station on a base that can move from side to side. The *Canadarm2* can grab and move pieces of the station, tools, and equipment during construction.

Pieces of the station are made on Earth ▲ and shipped to space.

The finishing touches are made to a module ▶ at the Kennedy Space Center in Florida.

The Canadarm2 *is 60 feet (18 meters) ▶▶ long—about as long as a line of four cars stopped at a traffic light.*

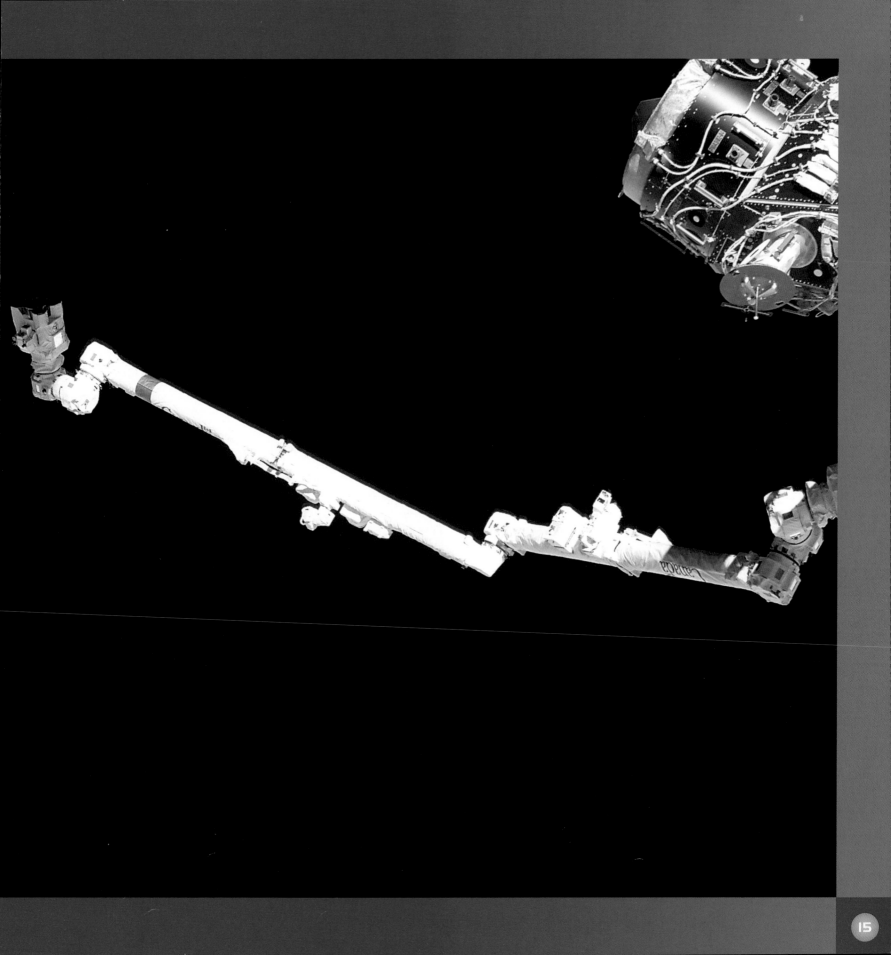

The Crew

When the ISS is complete, a crew of six or seven astronauts will be able to live there for up to six months. Today, crews are made up of two or three astronauts from both the United States and Russia, though astronauts from other countries have gone up in the past. Crews stay on the station for three to seven months. A space shuttle or *Soyuz* spacecraft brings a new crew to the station. Then it brings the old crew home to Earth.

New crew members are warmly ▶
greeted as they arrive at the station.

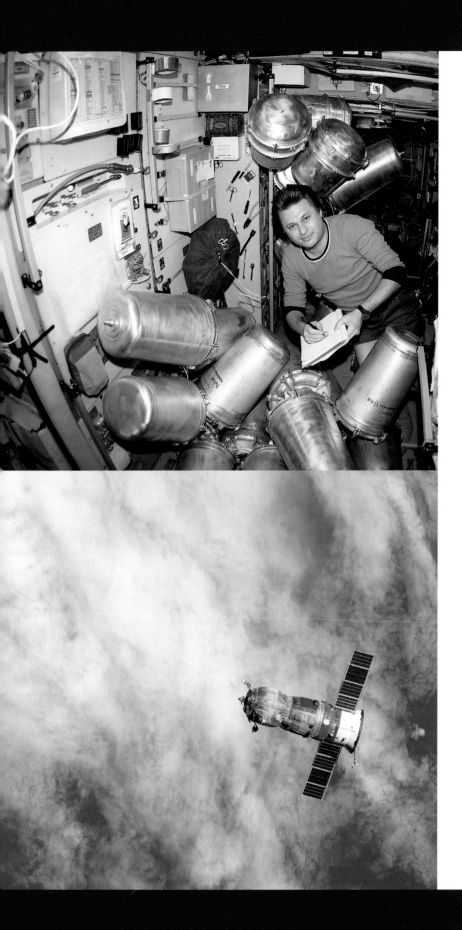

Because the crew is in space for a long time, they need a lot of supplies. New supplies are brought every time a new crew arrives. Supplies also are shipped in the Russian *Progress* spacecraft, which can travel without an astronaut. Supplies might include food, clothes, water, or small parts needed for experiments on the station. There is also an emergency spacecraft attached to the space station. The crew is always able to get home safely.

▲ *Russian astronaut Yury I. Onufrienko catalogs water canisters aboard the station.*

◄ *As well as bringing supplies, the Russian spacecraft* Progress 10 *takes trash away from the station. The trash will be burned up in the atmosphere.*

It takes about a year and a half for an astronaut to train to be part of the space station crew. The astronauts learn in classrooms in both the United States and Russia. They learn to speak English and Russian so they can talk to each other. They have medical training in case a crew member gets sick. They learn how to do the science experiments and work the robotic arm.

Part of the astronauts' job is to work outside the station in space. They practice for these space walks by working underwater. At the Johnson Space Center in Houston, Texas, astronauts work on a life-size model of the space station in a huge pool. This helps them know what it will be like working in space where gravity won't be holding them down.

Often, when an astronaut first arrives at the station, he or she might feel "space sick" for a few days. Space sickness is a lot like feeling seasick on a boat. Astronauts feel as if they are going to throw up. After a few days, their bodies feel normal again.

Astronauts train underwater at the largest ▶
indoor swimming pool in the world.

Work to Do

The most important job of the crew each day is to keep the space station in good shape. They test the systems, work on the computers, and make sure the spacecraft is running smoothly. Every day, the crew communicates with Mission Control, the people on Earth in charge of the ISS. They talk by radio or by e-mail.

The crew does experiments on the station that can't be

Astronauts work on the equipment in the Destiny *laboratory.*

Mission Control in Korolev, Russia, keeps in daily contact with crew members up in space.

done on Earth. They watch how metal or fire acts differently in space. They grow crystals that will help scientists on Earth understand and cure diseases. They see how plants will grow in space. Many of their experiments are done in the Microgravity Science Glovebox.

This is a large clear box with gloves attached to one side. It keeps liquids or other materials from floating around the station during an experiment.

The crew members also perform experiments on

▼ *Astronaut Pedro Duque of Spain works on an experiment in the Microgravity Science Glovebox.*

themselves. They study how living in space affects their bones, blood, heart, muscles, and other parts of their bodies. Because they float most of the time, they don't use their muscles enough. All of their muscles, even their hearts, get weaker. Bones lose some of their strength, too. The astronauts study their bodies to find ways to stay healthy and strong during long periods of time in space.

Astronaut Edward T. Lu takes a picture out of the window of the Zvezda *Service Module.*

The crew also studies Earth. From their windows, they can watch and take pictures of the oceans, cities, deserts, forests, and even stormy cloud patterns.

Outside the station, the crew takes space walks to construct parts of the station. The astronauts wear special space suits. There is no air in space, so the suit has a pack filled with oxygen for the astronaut to breathe. It also

has a light on the helmet
for when the sun sets.
Inside the helmet, there is
a radio so that the astronaut
can talk to the crew inside
the station at all times.

During these space
walks, the astronauts are
always attached to the
space station by a long
cable, or tether. Just in
case, they also wear a
backpack that has jets to
power them back to the
station so they don't float
off into space.

◀ *An astronaut on a space walk works
outside the station.*

Daily Life

★ Life on the space station is not just work. The crew also reads books, listens to music, or plays chess or cards. They talk with or e-mail friends and family on Earth. The crew must exercise a few hours every day to keep their bones and muscles strong. The station has an exercise bike, a treadmill, and other machines. Special straps and harnesses keep the astronauts on the machines as they work out.

Even with very little water on the station, crew

A vacuum sucks up the clippings ▶ as this astronaut gets a haircut.

members still take showers and brush their teeth every day. However, there is not enough water on the space station for the crew to do laundry. So they wear their clothes three days or more before changing. They change their underwear and socks every other day. When they have to go to the bathroom, they use a special toilet with handles for their hands and feet to keep them from floating around.

The crew on the ISS eats three meals a day. Just like you, they might have eggs, cereal, and orange juice for breakfast. They might have peanut butter, pears, and lemonade for lunch and chicken, rice, and apple cider for dinner.

The ISS does not have a refrigerator, so they cannot keep any food that can spoil.

▼ *Many foods are specially packaged for the astronauts.*

Meals on the International Space Station are a mix of American and Russian foods, so that everyone gets a little taste of home.

Many of the foods come in cans or pouches. Crew members may need to add water to some of the foods, such as green beans, before they can eat them. They heat foods in a special food warmer. All of the drinks come as a powder and need water added, too. Some foods, such as nuts or cookies, can be eaten right out of the bag.

The crew sits together at a small table that pulls down from the wall. They have to hold on to their trays or the food will float all around the station!

Mealtimes are a lot of fun ▼
aboard the space station.

Space Station Lessons

✦ It is hard for the crew to live so high above Earth without their family and friends, but life on the International Space Station is an adventure. As the station orbits Earth, the crew gets a view of their home, and of outer space, that we never get down below.

The ISS will help scientists know how long it is safe for people to live in space. The space station is practice for longer missions. It helps scientists know if people could ever make it as far as

◄ *Crew members can get homesick for family and friends on Earth.*

the planet Mars and back. It helps us know if a crew could ever live for a long time on a permanent space station on the moon or Mars. The space station may also be a place where large spacecraft can be built. It would cost less to launch a ship from space than it does from Earth.

The International Space Station teaches both the crew, and those of us watching from Earth, about ourselves. It takes teamwork between nations to build the largest spacecraft ever made. Working together makes the world, and space, a better place to live.

A view of the International Space Station under construction ▷

Glossary

crew—the people who work together on a spacecraft

microgravity—the feeling of weightlessness in space

probes—small spacecraft, without astronauts, sent to study the moon or planets

robotic—run by machines and computers

solar—run by energy from the sun

space walks—short trips outside the station in space

tether—a cable that clips onto an astronaut's space suit and works like a leash to keep him or her from floating off into space

Did You Know?

• The 16 countries that will play an important part in building the International Space Station are Belgium, Brazil, Canada, Denmark, France, Germany, Italy, Japan, the Netherlands, Norway, Russia, Spain, Sweden, Switzerland, the United Kingdom, and the United States.

• Two members of the crew of the fourth mission to the station, called Expedition Four, spent the longest time in space. Carl Walz (1955–) and Dan Bursch (1957–) spent 196 days away from Earth.

• After meals, cleanup is easy. There is no dishwasher. The trays and trash are stored. When a space shuttle arrives, the trash is put in the shuttle and brought back to Earth. Or, if it is put into a Russian *Progress,* it burns up in Earth's atmosphere.

• Astronauts aren't always the only ones in the space station. A few space tourists have come aboard for short vacations. Dennis Tito, a California businessman, became the first visitor in 2001. He trained for six months before takeoff and spent millions of dollars to pay for the trip.

Want to Know More?

AT THE LIBRARY

Branley, Franklyn M. *The International Space Station*. New York: HarperCollins, 2000.

Cole, Michael D. *International Space Station: A Space Mission*. Springfield, N.J.: Enslow, 1999.

Editors of *YES Mag*. *The Amazing International Space Station*. Toronto: Kids Can Press, 2003.

Graham, Ian. *The Best Book of Spaceships*. New York: Kingfisher, 1998.

ON THE WEB

For more information on the **International Space Station,** use FactHound to track down Web sites related to this book.

1. Go to www.facthound.com
2. Type in a search word related to this book or this book ID: **0756508525**.
3. Click on the *Fetch It* button.

Your trusty FactHound will fetch the best Web sites for you!

ON THE ROAD

National Air and Space Museum
Sixth and Independence Avenue Southwest
Washington, DC 20560
202/357-2700
To learn more about the solar system and space exploration

The Kansas Cosmosphere and Space Center
1100 N. Plum
Hutchinson, KS 67501
800/397-0330
To see a large collection of spacecraft and a detailed history of space flight through time

Kennedy Space Center
Visitor Complex
Kennedy Space Center, FL 32899
321/452-2121
To see exhibits on the history of space flight and even catch a shuttle launch

NASA Goddard Space Flight Center
Visitor Center
Code 130
Greenbelt, MD 20771
301/286-9041
To see exhibits of NASA's many space missions

Index

◄ **About the Author:** *Dana Meachen Rau loves to study space. Her office walls are covered with pictures of planets, astronauts, and spacecraft. She also likes to look up at the sky with her telescope and write poems about what she sees. Ms. Rau is the author of more than 100 books for children, including nonfiction, biographies, storybooks, and early readers. She lives in Burlington, Connecticut, with her husband, Chris, and children, Charlie and Allison.*